Take,
Eat and
Drink

Take, Eat and Drink

THIRTEEN
COMMUNION
MEDITATIONS

C.S.S. Publishing Co.
Lima, Ohio

TAKE, EAT AND DRINK

LIBRARY OF CONGRESS
Library of Congress Cataloging-in-Publication Data

Take, eat, and drink : thirteen communion meditations.
p. cm.
ISBN 1-566-73109-4
1. Communion sermons. 2. Sermons, American.
BV4257.5.T35 1989 88-21701
252'.6—dc19 CIP

9820 / ISBN 1-55673-109-4 PRINTED IN U.S.A.

Table of Contents

ONE

Eating at the King's Table

2 Samuel 9:1-11

[King David said] "Mephibosheth, your master's son, shall always eat at my table." (v. 10b)

Are you a people watcher?

I am. The most interesting thing about going to the State Fair is the chance to watch people. In fact, I find them more interesting than the livestock. Except for size and color, every cow looks and acts like every other cow, and every pig looks and sounds like every other pig.

But that's not true with people!

I sat one day for about ten minutes waiting for a dental appointment. There were three other people in the waiting room. One was a middle-aged man who was evidently reading a business report or a research paper, for his lips were moving as he absorbed the contents. He never looked up. A young man kept flipping through the pages of some magazines stacked on a table beside him, glancing shyly around between pick-ups. An elderly woman tried to avoid looking at any of the three of us; maybe because she felt outnumbered. I sat there and did three character studies.

I do this same thing when I read Scriptures: I watch people. The list of names is interesting when you dream about the personal history that may be behind each name listed. For example, in the last chapter of Philippians Paul pleads with Euodia and Syntyche, two women in the church at Philippi, to please try to get along with each other. That is all he says, but just sit and watch those two women in your imagination, and you can almost see some of the enmity (maybe unfounded) they had for each other.

The Bible is not just stories about saints. It is full of personal histories of folk exactly like us. That's the reason it is a grand place to people-watch.

There is a man mentioned in the Old Testament whose story always makes me think of the Lord's Table and the privilege each of us has in being invited to that Table. He is mentioned four times in the second book of Samuel: when he was five years old, when he was a young man, when someone misinterpreted his actions, and when he was given an inheritance. His name was Mephibosheth.

We have to know something about his father and his grandfather in order to know and understand his circumstances. His grandfather was Saul, king of Israel. His father was Jonathan, Saul's beloved son. The Israelites were at war with the Philistines. Saul and Jonathan, and two of Saul's other sons, went out to fight. The Israelites lost the battle and there was a wholesale slaughter: the king and his sons were killed.

When the news of the defeat got back to the capitol, the nurse of Jonathan's five-year-old son took the boy and fled from the city. As she was running, she dropped the child and the fall permanently crippled him in both feet.

David was made the next king of Israel, and since Saul had threatened David's life and pushed him into exile, Mephibosheth's nurse was fearful that the new king might destroy any remaining member of Saul's family. So she kept the boy in hiding and she told him, as he grew older, that he lived under a threat.

Because of his diplomacy, David was able to establish peace. Israel was no longer at war with any of her surrounding countries. And one day David began to wonder if any member of Saul's family was still living. He discovered, through one of Saul's former servants, that there was a grandson: a crippled young man living in obscurity in a little town about twenty-five miles south of Jerusalem.

David sent for Mephibosheth. The young man was frightened. He thought his life was in danger. So he hobbled into the king's court, expecting to hear the death sentence. But instead he heard: "Mephibosheth, you shall live here with me as one of my sons, and eat at my table."

Mephibosheth couldn't believe what he heard. "You are going to be kind to me?" he asked the king. "Should a king show kindness to a dead dog like me?"

"Yes," answered King David. "You shall sit at my table." And Mephibosheth did. "From that time on, he ate regularly with the king, as though he were one of his sons." (2 Samuel 9:1-11)

I watched this story re-enacted some years ago. A thirty-year-old Presbyterian minister received a call to become the pastor of a local church. He had already served two churches in our state since graduation from seminary. There were some marital difficulties which resulted in separation and finally divorce. Richard resigned from the church he was serving when this happened, and for the next three years worked as a salesman. But he yearned to return to the ministry and let that yearning be known in the Presbyterian circles.

A church in Louisville, Kentucky, interviewed him but felt it could not accept a divorced minister. A church in Tennessee gave him a call, but the Knoxville presbytery turned him down because of the divorce. And then a church in North Carolina found him acceptable, as well as the presbytery in that area. Richard had felt as though he would never again be acceptable because of the failure of his marriage. The church to which he was called gave him an assurance that he was, and he discovered that he had been invited to stay with the King and eat at his Table once more.

All of us are invited to stay with the King, and to eat at his Table. It should be a surprise to each of us to receive such an invitation, as it was a surprise to Mephibosheth, because most of us are crippled in some way: maybe in spirit, maybe in morals, maybe in commitment. But we are still treated as a child of the King.

Each time I take the bread and the cup in Holy Communion I am awed by the symbolism of that Sacrament. But what surprises me even more was the Master taking the towel and the basin that Thursday evening and washing the feet of those "crippled disciples." His acceptance of Judas with his greed, of Peter with his impulsiveness, of Nathanael with his questioning, of Thomas with his doubts, of James and John with their impulsive behavior — all make me aware that he accepts me even though I am often crippled in spirit.

I was standing in the emergency room of a hospital some years ago with an injured child when my eye caught a sign over the nurse's desk. It read: "I know I'm somebody 'cause God don't make no trash."

We are somebodies . . . somebodies who are invited to eat at the King's Table regardless of how crippled we may be.

— *Wallace H. Kirby*

TWO

The Life We Prize

Luke 9:23

> *[Jesus said] If any[one] would come after me, let [them] deny self and take up [their] cross daily and follow me.*

Our family was skiing in Colorado with some friends. I rode up a long chair lift with a stranger who turned to me saying, "The name's Clyde; I'm a plumber from California. I'm out here to meet women and have fun. What's your work?"

I answered, "Fire insurance," the response I frequently give when I want to have some fun with an unsuspecting stranger.

He questioned, "Fire insurance? Who do you work for?"

"The Lord," I responded.

"Who?"

"The Lord. I'm a preacher."

If we had not been fifty feet off the ground, Clyde would have jumped out of the chair. I reassured him, "Relax; enjoy the ride."

After a few moments of silence he asked, "Is there any hope for a guy like me?"

I answered, "Certainly." Then I simply described the wonderful time our family and friends were having because of the way Christ had built our lives and our relationships.

When we stood at the top of the lift, Clyde went left, I to the right. Clyde yelled, "You've given me a lot to think about!"

According to the words of Jesus in Luke 9:23, we find the life we prize, first, through self-denial; second, through self-surrender; and third, through self-discovery. As we prepare in these moments to celebrate holy communion, we seek to meet Christ and to hear his Word for our lives.

1. *Self-denial.* In me there is that which must die. Many of my attitudes, actions, desires, and thoughts dishonor God and stifle the life God desires to awaken within me. My very nature is to twist, to curve, and to bend events to my own benefit. This self-centeredness constitutes the most serious sin besetting me, for I rebel against God and distort life. So Jesus said, "Deny yourself." Jesus' words convict me; I am guilty of excluding Jesus from areas of my life where I harbor dishonesty, lust, and bitterness. To deny self primarily means to die to all within myself which is not consistent with the Word and the love of Christ.

Christ's call is that I be crucified with him so "it is no longer I who live, but Christ who lives in me." (Galatians 2:20) I have to be willing to go to the Cross in self-denial; I reluctantly do so. Even then I rationalize taking back my own schemes. When I compromise God's commandments, I leave a mark, often invisible, on everything I touch. But eventually these flaws show up as my apparently self-sufficient life begins to fall apart.

As Jesus emptied himself and went to the Cross, so I must die to all within myself which is not of him. Paul said, "If we have been united with him [Christ] in a death like his, we shall certainly be united with him in a resurrection like his." (Romans 6:5) Christ's call to deny self means to turn away from all that is less than God's best for me.

2. *Self-surrender.* Jesus calls me to take up my cross daily. This means to surrender myself to him, trusting him to forgive my sins and to strengthen my life. Such unconditional commitment to Christ is difficult because I want to keep control of my life; I don't want to entrust myself to Christ's

management. This self-surrender has to be "daily" because Christ looks for a consistently deeper giving of myself to him.

As self-denial is to die to sin, turning from my rebellious ways, so self-surrender is to live to Christ, obeying his will. Taking up my cross does not primarily refer to bearing problems and difficulties. It means identifying with Christ's way of sacrificial love for God and his people. In that commitment Christ gives me the strength to bear my burdens.

Jesus said, "For whoever would save his life will lose it; and whoever loses his life for my sake and the gospel's will save it." (Mark 8:35) In such self-surrender I find life handed back to me complete and promising. In committing myself to Christ amazing opportunities and new dimensions of strength open to me.

As we prepare to observe the Lord's Supper we remember how on the very night when Jesus initiated this sacrament, he prayed that God would take the cup of suffering from him. Then he prayed, "Nevertheless not my will, but yours, be done." (Luke 22:42) Here we see the act of self-surrender to which Christ gave himself and to which he calls us.

One evening when our two children were in junior high school, I made a special point to be home with my family. I am one who has to struggle to turn from the pressures of my work and to love my wife and children according to their needs. On that particular evening I decided to bless my family with my presence. In reality I needed them. With a magnanimous spirit I exclaimed, "I'll do the dishes."

Everyone shouted, "Great!" and disappeared.

"Count it all joy" (James 1:2), I kept telling myself as I got the dishwasher loaded and started.

Then our daughter Lynn remembered she needed some sewing material for a class in school the next morning. She asked, "Dad, could you take me to the store?"

"Oh sure," I answered, tugging on my snow boots.

When we returned, our son David pushed his page of math problems in front of me. They gave me a headache just to look at them. I reminded myself of Paul's admonition, "Be filled with the Spirit . . . always and for everything giving thanks." (Ephesians 5:18, 20)

Then I realized that it was garbage night. Thanks to Charlie and Martha Shedd who had conducted a family enrichment seminar at Covenant, I had accepted the assignment of putting the garbage out two nights a week. I went from bedroom to bedroom emptying the waste baskets and then dug the hair out of the bathroom sink drain, crawling under the kitchen table to get a discarded gum wrapper. Finally I got all that lovely stuff collected and out to the curb.

By then the evening was over; I had not played a game of checkers or anything else that I wanted to do. It would have been easier to have worked in my office. I felt sorry for myself. I went in to say good night to the kids. Lynn exclaimed, "Dad, it has been a wonderful evening!"

David said, "You do good work, Pops! I'm amazed at how patient you've been tonight."

Surprised, I gave thanks. Denying myself, surrendering myself in sacrificial love for others has never come easily for me. But that evening I caught a glimpse of the life I prize.

3. *Self-discovery.* Jesus said, ". . . and follow me." Jesus' call to discipleship involves self-denial, self-surrender, and self-discovery. In the Christian life we forfeit, commit, and find.

C. S. Lewis in his sermon, "The Weight of Glory," helps us see that to deny ourselves, to take up our crosses in order to follow Christ, does not mean we become zeros; we become more complete persons according to the loving plan of the Creator. We seek to attain to the maturity, stature, and "fulness of Christ." (Ephesians 4:13)

After the seige of Rome in 1849, Garibaldi, the Italian patriot proclaimed:

> *Soldiers, all our efforts against superior forces have been unavailing. I have nothing to offer but hunger, thirst, hardships, and death.*

Those Italian soldiers rose to the occasion, liberated their people, and established a nation.

In a similar manner, Christ's call to sacrificial commitment releases the heroic dimension of the human personality, giving ultimate consequence to our lives. The Spirit of God turns our weaknesses into strength, stiffens our resolve, and gives us courage to bring the hope of Christ to others.

At the Innsbruck Olympics in 1976, Bill Koch was a surprise winner of the silver medal in the grueling, thirty-kilometer cross-country ski event. Koch said he had the thrill to become an Olympian only through self-denial and commitment. So in the Christian life Paul said, "[We make] every thought captive to obey Christ." (2 Corinthians 10:5) The Christian life is a call to discipline, dedication, and discovery. "One thing I do . . . I press on toward the goal for the prize of the upward call of God in Christ Jesus." (Philippians 3:13, 14) Christ offers us the highest challenge for our living.

In the observance of the Lord's Supper we discover the life we prize as we die to the sin within us, as we surrender ourselves in trust to Christ's leading, and as we become alive to the full dimensions of the divine image in which we have been created. Paul writes, "We were buried therefore with him [Christ] by baptism into death, so that as Christ was raised from the dead by the glory of the Father, we too might walk in newness of life." (Romans 6:4)

A loving husband and wife adopted a baby boy. These new parents had died to themselves and had found life through loving the child entrusted to them. Their son, named Fred, grew strong in the riches of Christ's love. When Fred was in his twenties, he learned the identity of his natural father who remained a hateful person. Inner fear and hurt surged into Fred's spirit as he came to know the man who had been his father.

Then Fred learned that his natural father was dying from heart disease. He wanted nothing to do with his father who continued to be spiteful. Yet the son wanted to forgive and to be forgiven. Fred shared his struggle with his small group fellowship. They patiently helped him to give up his fears and hurts, entrusting himself to Christ. As Fred lived by faith in Christ, he loved his father by faith, seeing his father in the light of God's image no matter how dim that image seemed.

Through prayer, friends helped Fred to see himself going to his father and finding reconciliation. Fred finally went to his father's bedside. The son said, "Dad, I love you and I ask you to forgive me for any way in which I have hurt you."

The father shouted, "Why don't you go back to your fancy living and just leave me alone!" Fred had the choice of whether to quit and to give up or to go to the Cross and to die to any claims for himself. He identified with Jesus' humiliation and suffering. He went back again to a father who could only be more and more spiteful. Suddenly one day when Fred walked into the room, his father broke into tears. The father and son embraced for the first time in their lives.

The father said, "Son, I'm dying; I need help." During the days that followed the son was able to help his father come to know Jesus Christ and to trust him in life and death. Fred knew that his own strength had not enabled him to find reconciliation with his father. Fred had been able to deny himself, to surrender himself, and to discover the life he prized.

— James R. Tozer

THREE

The Rite of Remembrance

Luke 22:19

[Jesus] took bread, and when he had given thanks he broke it and gave it to them, saying, "This is my body which is given for you. Do this in remembrance of me."

"We are what we remember," wrote Dr. Ernest T. Campbell, the late pastor of the Riverside Church in New York City. The word remember came from two Latin words: "re" (back, again) and "memor" (mindful). To remember is to call an event, person, or thing back to mind again. It is to reassemble the members of a past event. The act of remembering affects our national life, our personal life, and our religious life. In our national life, for example, we have "Veterans' Day" when we reassemble in our minds the lives of the men and women who have served in the armed forces and express our gratitude for their sacrifices. In our personal life, we have a way of remembering what we ought to forget and of forgetting what we ought to remember. When a newspaper reporter interviewed a famous psychologist, he asked, "What do you try to do for a person who comes to you for treatment?" The psychologist answered, "Our objective in analysis is to free the patient from the tyranny of the past." Today, we consider the place of remembering in our religious life.

At Passover time in the springtime of the year A.D. 30, little clusters of Jewish men and women and children gathered all over the old city of Jerusalem to do what their ancestors had done for nearly thirteen centuries. They shared a meal together. Every Jewish meal was a religious occasion. Those meals began with the father of the family, or the rabbi with his pupils, or the host with his guests, taking bread into his hands, and saying, "Blessed art thou, O Lord our God, King of the universe, who brings forth bread from the earth." Then, the entire meal would follow. Cups of wine were taken during the meal. At the conclusion of the meal, there would be the final cup of wine called "The Cup of Blessing." Again, the father of the family, the rabbi with his pupils, the host with his guests, would take the cup of wine and say, "Blessed art thou, O Lord our God, King of the universe, who creates the fruit of the vine." Christ did this every time he sat down with his twelve ambassadors. On Thursday night, by our time reckoning (although it would have been Good Friday by Jewish reckoning, since the Jewish day begins at sunset), Christ did what he had done many times before. He took bread, he gave thanks, he broke the bread, and he gave it to them at the beginning of the meal. This time, however, he did something he never had done before. He identified the bread which he gave them with his body. Then, they had an entire meal. At the end of the meal, Christ took the Cup of Blessing, gave thanks, shared it with them, and said something he had never said before. As he gave them the cup, he said, "This is my blood of the new covenant." Then, he added these words: "Do this so that you will remember me." (Luke 22:19, Barclay) As Christians have reflected on that command, they have seen three dimensions in this Rite of Remembrance.

I

First of all, by means of this Rite of Remembrance, we are to do the remembering. Whenever Jewish people kept the Feast of Passover, they kept it as a way of remembering. In the Book of Exodus, it states: "For seven days you shall eat unleavened cakes, and on the seventh day there shall be a pilgrim-feast of the Lord. Only unleavened bread shall be eaten during the seven days; nothing fermented and no leaven shall be seen throughout your territory. On that day you shall tell your son. 'This commemorates what the Lord did for me when I came out of Egypt.' " (Exodus 13:6-8, NEB) Just as the Jewish Passover was a way for the individual Jew to remember God's great act of deliverance, so when Christians do this action Christ commanded, we remember the great act of deliverance wrought by God in Christ. In 1805 at Saint Paul's Cathedral, London, England, a funeral was held for the greatest naval hero in English history. There is a square in London called "Trafalger Square" which is named for the battle at which Lord Nelson distinguished himself. In October, 1805, Horatio Nelson's funeral was conducted in that magnificent house of worship. When the sailors who carried the coffin to its grave had finished their duty, they took the Union Jack flag from the coffin. A witness reported the scene this way: "With reverence and with efficiency, they lowered the body of the world's greatest admiral into its tomb. Then, as though answering to a sharp order from the quarterdeck, they all seized the Union Jack with which the coffin had been covered and tore it to fragments, and each took his souvenir of the illustrious dead." This piece of a flag became a memento, a souvenir, a means of remembering their hero. In the Rite of Remembrance which Christ gave us, something like that takes place, but in a far greater way. On that Thursday night "in which he was betrayed," Christ commanded us, saying, "Do this so that you will remember me." (Luke 22:19, Barclay) First of all, we are to remember.

II

Secondly, by means of this Rite of Remembrance, other people are to do the remembering. In Saint Paul's Letter to the Corinthians, he wrote: "Every time you eat this bread and drink the cup, you proclaim the death of the Lord, until he comes." (1 Corinthians 11:26, NEB) When we celebrate this Rite of Remembrance, we are not simply reminding ourselves of what Christ did. We are also reminding other people that they have a great value because of what Christ did for them. They are brothers "for whom Christ died."

Throughout the Old Testament, remembering played a powerful role in the history of the people. In Moses' farewell address, for example, he told them, "Be careful not to forget the Lord who brought you out of Egypt, out of the land of slavery." (Exodus 6:12, NEB) Physical reminders helped people to remember. The teaching of the commandments was to be bound to the forehead, to the arms, and to the posts of the doors. Such tangible signs play a part in stirring the memories of other persons. There was, for instance, a little girl who looked upon her mother as the most beautiful woman in the world. Often, she would say to her mother, "I love the beauty of your face and your eyes and your hair. But, thank God, Mother, that you wear gloves, because I can't stand to look at your hands. They are so scarred and ugly." Finally, the mother said to this little child, "Let me tell you what happened. When you were a little baby and slept in the nursery, a fire broke out in our house. I ran up the stairs and through the flames to your room. I picked you up and carried you out of that burning house. From that time on, my hands have looked like this." Those scars were a perpetual memorial for that little girl of her mother's love for her. Likewise, this great Sacrament of the Lord's Supper is a Rite of Remembrance by which the heart of the world is stimulated to recall the sacrifice of the Cross. By this action, wrote Saint Paul, "you proclaim the death of the Lord, until he comes."

III

Third, by means of this Rite of Remembrance, God is to remember. Recall the old story in the Book of Genesis about the rainbow. Why did God set the rainbow on the cloud? Speaking of the rainbow, God said to Noah, "This is the sign of the covenant which I establish between myself and you and every living creature with you, to endless generations:

My bow I set in the cloud,
sign of the covenant
between myself and earth.
When I cloud the sky over the earth,
the bow shall be seen in the cloud.

Then I will remember the covenant which I have made between myself and you and living things of every kind . . . The bow shall be in the cloud; when I see it, it will remind me of the everlasting covenant between God and living things on earth of every kind." (Genesis 9:12-16, NEB) The rainbow was to remind God of the covenant. Again, in the Book of Numbers, are these words: "When you go into battle against an invader and you are hard pressed by him, you shall raise a cheer when the trumpets sound, and this will serve as a reminder of you before the Lord your God and you will be delivered from your enemies . . . the trumpets shall be a reminder on your behalf before the Lord your God." (Numbers 10:9-10, NEB)

With this background from the Hebrew Scriptures in mind, think again of the Rite of Remembrance which Christ gave us that Thursday night in Jerusalem so long ago: "Do this so that you will remember me." We do this action commanded by Christ as a perpetual memorial to bring before God this representation of the great sacrifice of Christ on Calvary. In a great hymn written by a bishop of the Church of England, there is a clear statement of what this Rite of Remembrance means:

"And now, O Father, mindful of the love
That bought us once for all, on Calvary's tree,
And having with us him that pleads above,
We here present, we here spread forth to thee,
That only off'ring perfect in thine eyes,
The one true, pure, immortal sacrifice.

"Look, Father, look on his anointed face,
And only look on us as found in him;
Look not on our misusings of thy grace,
Our prayers so languid, and our faith so dim;
For lo! between our sins and their reward,
We set the passion of thy Son our Lord."

(The Hymnal 1940 According to the Use of the Episcopal Church, 189)

"For indeed our Passover has begun; the sacrifice is offered — Christ himself," wrote Saint Paul. (1 Corinthians 5:7, NEB) The old Passover of Israel was held in celebration of Israel's exodus from Egypt and entry into the land of Promise. In this Rite of Remembrance, Christ gave the new Israel, his Church, the new Passover to commemorate our exodus from the slavery of sin and our entry into the sphere of Christ's kingdom. Every time you take part in the Service of the Lord's Supper, you are recalling the dimensions of this Rite of Remembrance for ourselves, for other people, and for our Lord God: "May you be strong to grasp, with all God's people, what is the breadth and length and height and depth of the love of Christ." (Ephesians 3:18, NEB)

— *Edward Chinn*

FOUR

The Miracle Comes at the Breaking

Luke 24:13-16, 28-31, 35

Then they told what had happened on the road, and how he was known to them in the breaking of the bread. (v. 35)

After his resurrection, Jesus promised that he would be with us everywhere. We can be assured and conscious of his presence in the private place of prayer, but also the rush of daily routines, including a classroom or a crowded restaurant; or even in the midst of a rabid crowd at a sports event.

But without a doubt there are circumstances and settings where we are more likely to meet our Lord, or where his presence is more intimately experienced. Our Scripture lesson for this day illustrates what I'm trying to say.

It was late afternoon and evening of the first Easter. Two followers of Jesus were walking a slow and sorrowing seven miles from Jerusalem to the village of Emmaus. By our usual view of things, they were not famous or important people. The one is identified as Cleopas, and we know nothing more about him nor do we learn more of him later in the Scriptures; the other is not even named. But they had loved Jesus very much and had followed him earnestly in their own relatively insignificant way. Now Jesus was gone, and they were desperately lonely, afraid and unsure of themselves and of the future.

So they walked a forsaken, dusty road, reminiscing and questioning. They recalled those happier days when Jesus was among them, teaching and healing. They pondered with pain the kaleidoscope of the past few days. They asked themselves the meaning of all that had happened, and found no answer.

Suddenly a Stranger joined in their walk and their talk. He came so quietly that he seemed no intrusion to their private pain. He asked them why they were so troubled, then went on to explain the Scriptures with which they had been wrestling so helplessly. When they arrived at their destination, the Stranger acted as if he were going on. But when the two men invited him to stay, he quickly accepted their invitation.

As they sat at the table, the Stranger took bread, blessed it, and broke it for distribution. In that moment, the New Testament says, "their eyes were opened," and they knew it was their Lord.

After Jesus was gone from them, one of the men said that they should have recognized Jesus when they were walking and talking, because of the way their "hearts burned" within them as he explained the Scriptures to them. But the revelation came at a different moment. As they told it later to the disciples, Jesus "was known to them in the breaking of the bread."[1] It was at that moment when he took the bread and broke it that they knew he was their Lord.

That's surprising, isn't it? Logic says that they should have recognized Jesus while he was explaining the Scriptures. They themselves reasoned so. Their hearts had burned with excitement as he interpreted the passages to them; that should have been indication enough that this Stranger was their Lord. The preacher in me wishes it were so, for I open the Scriptures each week in the fond hope that people will, at such a moment, see their Lord. And often, of course, they do; for this is the purpose of the Scriptures and the expectation in preaching, that as the Scriptures are explained, people will see and experience Jesus Christ.

Come to think of it, we might have expected that the two men would have recognized Jesus at the moment he joined

[1] Luke 24:35 (RSV)

them. That event had about it the flash of recognition, what some might call the experiential moment. It's the kind of instance when you expect a miracle: two people walking in loneliness and need, talking about their Lord, and lo, he appears. And of course, they recognize him. But it didn't happen that way.

Instead, logical or not, Jesus was revealed to them when he broke the bread. Not in the dramatic appearance along the roadside, and not as he expounded the Scripture as only the Master Teacher could do, but when he took the common bread in his hands and broke it. "He was known to them in the breaking of the bread."

Why? What is it that made that moment so special, so revealing, so miraculous? Our first inclination is to think that when Jesus broke the bread the two men were reminded of what happened in the upper room, when Jesus instituted the sacrament of Holy Communion. But then we realize that this can't be the explanation, because these two men weren't present in the upper room, since they weren't part of the twelve.

Some have suggested that the two men were present when Jesus fed the multitude with the few loaves and fish. Thus they would remember the awesome moment when Jesus took a boy's luncheon loaf in hand, looked to his Father in prayer, and began to satisfy the hunger of a great crowd by the miracle of what happened to crumbs of bread under his touch. This is certainly possible, even likely. It's quite probable that these two men were part of the crowd on that special occasion, and if they were, they would no doubt have an indelible memory of the event.

But most of all, I think, it is that this act was so characteristic of Jesus. Often, over the years they had known and eaten with Jesus, they had seen him bless bread and break it, then distribute it to his friends. Often they had seen the strong carpenter hands wrench a piece of tough, middle-eastern bread for their enjoyment. Often he had fed them! Sometimes there was much and sometimes little; sometimes there was fish or lamb, sometimes fruit, sometimes neither. But always there was bread, and always the hands of their Lord, breaking it and blessing it.

It was not simply the physical act. It was that some quality of Jesus himself went into that act of breaking. Somehow Jesus was *invested* in the breaking. While the few loaves and fish remained whole in his hands, they fed no one. It was when he broke them that the multitudes were nourished. So, too, with every meal: the bread accomplished nothing lying on the table. It was when he broke it that the people at the table were fed.

And so it was, especially, in his own Person. Magnificent as he was, his value was slight if he held himself aloof, in majestic splendor. Come to think of it, they couldn't have imagined him doing so. It was when he was broken that he fed the multitudes: broken, daily, in the pain of his compassion and in the untiring way he gave of himself to their needs; and broken at last on Calvary, in the ultimate sacrifice.

I am intrigued by the way the breaking of the bread has for so long caught up believers. In the Roman Catholic Church, through the long centuries when the mass was celebrated in Latin, there was that sacred moment when the priest would lift the Host and speak the momentous words of our Lord: in the Latin, *Hoc est corpus meus* — "This is my Body . . ." Generations of the devout — and yes, of the superstitious, of course — waited for this moment and for the ringing of the bell. It was an exultant, mysterious moment, signaled by those special words. No wonder that the peasants, not knowing Latin, made the words into *hocus pocus*. Their corruption of the Latin became a phrase in our common speech, a popular "magic" incantation. They knew that moment as a peak of mystery, when something quite beyond them happened. Hocus pocus, indeed.

But believe me, the breaking of this bread is no "hocus pocus." It is a profound and magnificent mystery, but it is no clever magic. It is, rather, the very essence of who our Lord is, and of how he works. He came to our world to be broken. His body comes to us, not in sublime and delicate beauty, but *broken*. He makes us whole by himself being broken.

And as it is with the Master, so it is with his servants. The contemporary Roman Catholic mystic, Henri Nouwen, has given us a phrase which sums it up: *wounded healers.* You cannot really heal others, he reminds us, until and unless you are yourself a wounded person. It is from that wounded state that we best reach out to love, to touch, and to heal. If we stand off at a safe and antiseptic distance, we are of little use. It is as we ourselves are broken that we have the grace and the power to bring healing to others.

Surely this table to which we come today is a table for broken people. The broken bread of communion can never be received by those who think themselves to be whole. That's why the classic invitation to commune begins, "Ye that do truly and earnestly repent of your sins . . ." The invitation does not read, "You that are perfect," or "You that have been sanctified." As a matter of fact, it doesn't even say, "You that are saved." The invitation comes to those who know that they are sinners, and who want to be saved from their sins.

In a sense, there is a sign over this Table which reads, "For Sinners Only." Now in truth, that includes everyone, for all have sinned and come short of the glory of God. But of course it is effective only for those who can read it. That is, for those who can recognize and acknowledge that they are sinners.

Because, you see, we can't really take this broken Bread in a whole hand. It is only as we confess our own broken state — *our sins* — that we can receive such a gift of healing and forgiveness.

As you perhaps know, the Greek Orthodox Church refers to the service of Holy Communion as the Eucharist, which means the giving of thanks. But Professor Dale Bruner reminds us that the word means more than that. He notes that *eu* means *good*, and that *charis* is the root for our English word *Caress.* So it is, Dr. Bruner says, that "the Lord's Supper is the good caress. In that sacrament God comes spiritually and physically and touches us, and He says, 'I love you.' "[2]

The late, great British preacher, Leslie Weatherhead, always remembered a boyhood experience of a special friend of his. The friend's father was a great man and, unfortunately, his work took him away from home on many occasions. The boy missed his father dearly and looked forward with great excitement to each time when his father returned.

However, one night when the father was expected home from a journey, the boy faced a huge disappointment. He had been naughty and had been sent to bed early, before his father's return. He awakened between ten and eleven that night and heard his father's voice downstairs in conversation. Fearfully, he dressed and came down. He expected a rebuke, for he knew he was disobeying in what he was doing. But his father took him into his arms and held him very close, so close that the boy could feel the beat of his father's heart. And the father said simply, "My own little child."[3]

I'm sure that's what our Heavenly Father wants to say to you and to me today. We come, knowing that we are broken. Sin and the ravages of daily life have left their marks on our minds, our spirits, and our psyches. We look at the majesty of God and the purity of our Lord Christ and feel that we have no right to approach such perfection.

But then we encounter the miracle of the *breaking*. "This is my Body," our Lord says, "which is *broken* for you." And then, a voice of love, the Father's voice: "My own little child."

Come, dear friends, whatever your brokenness may be, and experience the miracle which is in the breaking.

— ***J. Ellsworth Kalas***

[2] F. Dale Bruner, *Christianity Today*, 11-4-85, p. 47.

[3] Leslie Weatherhead, "Suppose You Met Jesus," *Twenty Centuries of Great Preaching,* (Waco: Word books, 1971), Vol. XI, p. 135.

FIVE

The Woman at the Well

John 4:1-42

Jesus [said to the Samaritan woman], "If you knew the gift of God, and who it is who is saying to you, 'Give me a drink,' you would have asked him and he would have given you living water." (v. 10)

When Jesus met the woman at the well the encounter was a communion event. The element — the outward and visible sign of an inward and spiritual grace — was not what Jesus gave to the woman but what the woman gave to Jesus. What made this element, this object, a sacrament, a communion, was the way in which Jesus impacted the element with spirit, opening its and his meaning to her.

The element was a drink of water. Now, when used in the Sacrament of Baptism we would call this a formal sacrament. But as it was the water was a symbol which radiated its meaning from the beginning of the story to the end. We are all aware that water is heavily laden with symbolic meaning. It signifies to us that which is life-giving, cleansing, life-growth in plants and human beings, and all sorts of personal renewal. When touched by Jesus this drink of water became a sacramental event, communicating back to her the indwelling spirit of God which is what Jesus had to give to the woman.

If the transaction had been direct, we could see the offering, the gift by Jesus instantly conveying the inward spirit to the woman. As it was, the woman — clever in her own way — fended off Jesus' gift until he prevented any further evasion. The story describes several stages of communi*cation* before comm*union* took place. The "outward sign" which was a drink of water (now as sacramental symbol) required time before it opened itself to her as "inward grace." Jesus had to break through a determined, hard-minded, and defensive woman. Let's take a brief look at the progressions in their meeting.

1. Jesus asked her to give him a drink. Her reply indicated that the little knowledge she possessed was a dangerous thing. By her answer she sought to divert a genuine encounter with Jesus. "How is it that you, a Jew, ask a drink of water of me, a woman of Samaria?" What she is really saying is "You should know better than that. You don't really think I'm worthy of giving you water." But Jesus was not put off by her cockiness or defensiveness.

2. Jesus then challenged her with the implication of their encounter. "If you knew the gift of God, you would have asked him and he would give you living water." In her blunt, literal fashion, well-armored against anything that would disturb the status quo of her life, she reminded him that he had nothing with which to draw. She passed right over the distinction between the water she could give and "living" water. She either did not hear or did not want to hear. Her own intransigence blocked her in while all along she thought that she was cleverly blocking Jesus. "Are you greater than Jacob who gave us this well?" In saying this she put Jesus on notice that she knew a thing or two. "How clever I am; I know all about this well and its importance to us." Once more a little knowledge became a dangerous thing, holding her back from new experiences and knowledge.

3. Jesus moved on. "Every one who drinks of this water will thirst again, but whoever drinks of the water that I shall give him will never thirst; the water that I shall give him will

become in him a spring of water welling up to eternal life.'' Jesus caught her off guard, and, in her characteristic way she came back with a literal view. ''Give me this water, that I may not thirst, nor come here to draw.'' If she had the water Jesus offered, she would not need to work any further to obtain drink. She would actually be in control of her life, even as she fancied herself to be in control.

We see a pattern emerging. Everything the woman said to Jesus was an effort to justify her life. Was it selfishness? Ignorance? Lack of intelligence? I don't think so. She must have been fairly well put together or she would not have lasted as long as she had; but, she was extremely self-protective. In every instance she managed to put a barrier between her and a confrontation with Jesus and his gift. To evade receiving the communion he was doing his best to offer took all her skills.

4. Jesus, sensing these qualities in her, moved in closer. ''Go, call your husband.'' She: ''I have no husband.'' Jesus: ''You are right; you have had five husbands, and he whom you now have is not your husband.'' Now we can understand why she was so defensive, resisting every attempt by Jesus to touch her life. She had had to be such a woman, or else she would have ''gone under'' years before. This was her way of fighting off things that threatened her management of the narrow segment of life she carved out as her own.

At last Jesus got her attention. ''Certainly,'' she said, ''you are a prophet.'' Then, as though she had opened too wide, she instructed Jesus again. ''Our fathers worshiped on this mountain; you say Jerusalem is the only place to worship.'' Her ability to keep everything and everyone at arm's length was still at work. But this time, that which had preserved her life came to the end of its usefulness. She was in the presence of the Truth of God in Jesus. Here was someone mightier than all her little offerings and posturings. Her virtue in self-preservation became a flaw when it stood between her and Jesus. Only as she surrendered this virtue could the communion take place. Her inward spirit had to be transformed to receive the inward spirit which Jesus intended in this sacramental event.

5. Jesus is impatient. "Believe me, the hour is coming when neither on this mountain nor in Jerusalem will you worship the Father. You worship what you do not know; we worship what we know, for salvation is from the Jews. But the hour is coming and now is, when the true worshipers will worship the Father in spirit and truth, for such the Father seeks to worship him. God is spirit, and those who worship him must worship in spirit and in truth."

Jesus had cut through to the quick of her character, revealing her to be a confused, self-assertive person, picking up a bit of street wisdom here and there and concluding that the little she happened to know was all that she needed to know. However, the time had come for her to know that a better way of looking at life was confronting her. In effect he was saying that she could not go on as she had been. What had worked for her would no longer work now that she had met the Lord. The hour is coming for spirit (the inward gift Jesus was offering) and truth (the knowledge that Jesus gave). Only those who cast aside their pretenses at spirit and truth and receive that which God gives can worship him truly.

For the first time she displayed an innocent openness. "I know that the Messiah is coming (he who is called the Christ); when he comes he will show us all things." Once bereft of her defenses, she is in a position to know in spirit and in truth.

Jesus moved into his advantage. *"Not* the future, but *now!"* He said to her, "I who speak to you are he." Amazed that he had told her these things, and, as yet unable to compute them all, she ran to tell the people in the village. The people came to the well and invited Jesus to stay with them. He accepted the invitation.

Then it was they believed because of his word. "It is no longer because of your words," they say to the woman, "that we believe, for we have heard for ourselves, and we know that this is indeed the Savior of the world." Her testimony had brought them to Jesus, but it was their meeting with him in person that brought them to believe.

"We have heard for ourselves! We now know!" Communion had come to pass. The inward spirit which was Jesus' to give had been transmitted through this curious, strong-willed, yet misguided woman (who had, herself, become a sacramental object) until it enabled her friends to hear for themselves and to know.

Jesus had touched the gift of the water and transformed it into a sacramental event so that his grace was imparted to her and by her testimony into the lives of her fellows.

In the Christian tradition there are several elements which Scripture brings to us as formal objects for use in Sacraments — bread, wine, and water. Other traditions enlarge the number of elements used in additional Sacraments. But, in the world, the number of objects through which God communicates his spirit and truth are innumerable. Through them we can carry on a dialogue with Jesus as he moves us from self-defensiveness to surrender.

"But, Lord, I know all about money. I earn it. I control what it does. It represents me. I can give a little away, and through it I can be secure." Jesus keeps confronting us until we see his presence in the "element" which is money. It has the potential to bring about communion with him when used as a sacramental object. At last, pushing aside all our excuses, we recognize that he is speaking in and through it. His spirit prevails, and we become stewards of Christ.

"Lord, I know all about my talents. I was given them at birth. They are mine to exploit. I nursed them along; now I profit wisely from them. They will get me what I really deserve out of life." But Jesus persists in confronting us. He refuses all excuses and explanations until at last he speaks to us in and through our talents. We know that from then on we are to speak his meaning to the world through our talents. Our talents touched by him to be sacramental objects, become his.

There are innumerable objects around us that have the potential to be used by him as sacramental elements to reach into our lives and redeem us. From year to year as we hear the good news of Christ we are brought closer and closer to self-awareness as he pushes us ever nearer to the brink of communion with him.

— *Thomas D. Peterson*

SIX

More Real Than Food

John 6:51-55; 16:25a

The Jews . . . disputed among themselves, saying, "How can this man give us his flesh to eat?" So Jesus said to them, "Truly, truly, I say to you, unless you eat the flesh of the Son of man and drink his blood, you have no life in you." (vv. 52-53)

There are many who frown upon the celebration of Christmas because of its historical association with the pagan festival of Saternalia. It is true that the early Christian church decided to celebrate the birth of Christ on December 25 not because of any concrete evidence for that date, but in order to *replace* the popular Roman festival with a Christian festival. Christians felt that they had a new and more profound reason to celebrate during this season when the daylight hours gradually begin to lengthen.

In recent years a growing number of critics seem to be taking delight in an attempt to discredit Christianity by pointing out the ways in which many features of Christian belief and practice appear to be "borrowed" from the various mystery religions and other cults that were prevalent at and before the time of Jesus. Their assumption seems to be that if the ideas are "typical" or "borrowed" or "primitive," they are therefore also invalid at worst, or, at best, highly suspect.

What these critics fail to realize is that most ideas are built in one way or another on previous ideas and notions. You don't get at the essence of a teaching or thought by simply tracing it back to its most primitive roots or by reducing it to its lowest common denominator. For example, *sacrifice* is not necessarily a primitive notion and not all kinds of sacrifice are the same. There is a world of difference between sacrificing human infants to appease the gods and sacrificing one of your kidneys as a transplant for your ailing sister. It's what you do with the idea and reality of sacrifice that counts.

Various religious traditions clearly did color the development of Christian faith and theology. Many of the sayings attributed to Jesus himself, for instance, are direct quotes from the rabbinic literature which the contemporaries of Jesus knew well. A number of the extremely other-worldly, supernatural "mystery religions" of that time frequently used the imagery of "dying and rising gods," and rather primitive ideas about eating and drinking the body and blood of the gods were actually rather common.

The fact is that our current practice and celebration of Holy Communion has a variety of roots. We need to be aware of those roots, but ultimately it is the plant and the fruit that matters most. We must study the theological background of the Sacrament but, more important, we need to become clear about what Holy Communion has come to mean for us here and now.

Have you ever wondered about the background of some of the common expressions that we use in colloquial English? For example, where do we get the expression "dressed to the nines"? There are at least three possible explanations: One is that the Number 9 uniform was the most elegant dress uniform of British officers. A second possibility is that in some systems of numerology, the number three is a perfect number, a trinity, and since three three's would be a trinity of trinities it would symbolize absolute perfection. A third possible explanation would be that a complete bolt of cloth is nine yards, and if one uses the whole nine yards to make a garment the person wearing such an outfit would be dressed to perfection.

Similarly, the origin of the expression "mind your P's and Q's" is also cloudy. Some say it is a shortened form of "mind your please and your thanques." Others trace it back to the pubs where patrons would tell the bartender to mind the difference between a Pint and a Quart. Still others suggest that the reference is to typesetters having to be careful not to mix up the letters p and q. Others see it as a reference taken from the technical language of the ballet.

And since I mentioned Christmas at the outset, I think it would also be appropriate to list some of the theories as to why a theatrical flop is called a turkey. One has it that since people would go to any dumb show in the holiday season between Thanksgiving and Christmas, theater managers would not worry much about the quality of their shows after Thanksgiving. Hence, a mediocre show is a turkey. A quite different explanation holds that theatrical flops are called turkeys because Thanksgiving Day is traditionally the worst day of the entire year for getting people out to the theater. A third theory simply follows the stereotype that maligns the turkey as one of God's dumbest creatures.

We may never know the exact origins of these three expressions, but we do clearly know what they mean to us now.

The Sacrament of Holy Communion does likewise indeed have a variety of roots, a complex background of possible interpretations. In 1 Corinthians 11, Jesus describes the bread as his body, but the wine is described as "the cup of the new covenant in my blood." This earliest written version of the words of institution does not suggest the drinking of blood and is, therefore, very much in keeping with the Jewish Kosher tradition which forbids any kind of eating or drinking of blood! If we follow this tradition today, we present the cup to one another by saying simply "the cup of the new covenant" or "the cup of blessing." In Luke's account of the Last Supper the cup is simply referred to as "the fruit of the vine." In the Gospel of John there is *no* reference to Holy Communion at the Last Supper, but there is instead the account of Jesus washing his disciples' feet and a long discourse on a variety of topics, ending with the observation in John 16:25 that Jesus had been teaching everything in metaphors, in figures of speech.

There is, however, clear imagery of drinking the blood of Jesus in Matthew and Marks' accounts of the upper room: "Drink of it all of you; for this is my blood of the (new) covenant." Following tradition it is certainly appropriate to present the cup to one another with the words "The blood of Christ."

Surprisingly, the most blatant imagery of drinking the blood and eating the body of Jesus comes to us not in the stories of the Last Supper but in the sixth chapter of John's Gospel — in the story of the miraculous feeding of the multitude. It is here that John pictures Jesus as launching into the stark imagery of eating his flesh and blood as *real* food and drink! (Some early critics even accused the first Christians of practicing cannibalism as a part of their "sacred mysteries"!)

The key to understanding this striking language about the eating and drinking of Jesus' body and blood is to be found in the uniquely Christian emphasis that both *body* and *spirit*, both material and spiritual things, are equally important. At a loss for words to express the nature of the Christian hope, Saint Paul describes resurrection in terms of a "spiritual body" in 1 Corinthians 15. The material reality of flesh and blood is profoundly important. And yet Jesus offers something that is even more real, more important than flesh and blood. The sense of what Jesus says in John 6:51-55 is this: "My body is *more real* than flesh; my blood is *more real* than any earthly drink!"

The great theologian Paul Tillich put it this way: The Sacrament is not *Just* a symbol - it is a concrete *participation* in the spiritual reality of God's grace. The metaphors used by Jesus and the Gospel writers are much more than mere metaphors! They remind us of all the ways in which there is more to life than meets the eye, without downplaying the importance of the physical element.

The poet Herb Brokering wrote a hymn in 1984 to be sung to the tune of Beethoven's famous Ode To Joy from the Ninth Symphony, a hymn that beautifully expresses the value of each and every form of life, physical and spiritual:

God of concrete, air and fishes,
Pour our cup and break our bread;
Multiply our deepest wishes
'Til all want is felt and fed.
Princes, paupers, royal children
All in need of God's embrace;
Saints and angels feast on mercy,
Earth and heaven feast on grace.

Whatever its varied roots, Holy Communion has become a profound form of assurance that we can be filled with the love and grace of God in the name of Jesus, the Christ.

— ***Carl L. Jech***

SEVEN

Strength to Overcome Suffering

Romans 5:3-5

We rejoice in our sufferings, knowing that suffering produces endurance, and endurance produces character, and character produces hope, and hope does not disappoint us, because God's love has been poured into our hearts through the Holy Spirit which has been given to us.

Recently a letter came from a man who had lost his job. Though he faced discouragement and uncertainty, he refused to give in to despair. In his letter to me he said, "I feel as low as ever in my life, but I know this is not the final word. Because I believe God has work that he wants me to do, I rejoice and rely upon his guidance!"

This man had discovered the key to personal strength — the faith that God will work through every event in our lives to accomplish his perfect purpose for us. Such faith inspired Paul to exclaim, "We rejoice in our sufferings." (Romans 5:3)

As we prepare to celebrate the Lord's Supper, we expect to meet Christ in a fresh and intimate way in this sacrament. We seek strength from Christ so that we can overcome suffering and become an encouragement to other people.

To "rejoice in sufferings," as Paul did, seems contrary to our inclination. When sickness or business failure stagger us, how can we rejoice in such agony?

Having given the basis of Christian assurance in the first four chapters of Romans, Paul concluded in Romans 5:1, "Therefore, since we are justified by faith, we have peace with

God through our Lord Jesus Christ." Paul was saying that as we trust what Christ has done for us through his death and resurrection, we find a right relationship with God. We become confident of the purpose God has for us. (Romans 5:2) Such faith inspired Paul to exclaim, "We rejoice in our sufferings."

During this time of communion with Christ today, we can find confident joy amid our sufferings as we become strengthened in purpose, steadfast in perspective, and stable in personality.

1. *Become strengthened in purpose.* Jesus faced the most severe suffering for us. We remember how his body was broken for us as we take and eat the bread of Holy Communion. We remember how his blood was shed for us as we drink the cup. As God worked his purpose through Christ's sufferings, so we trust God to work his purpose for us through our sufferings.

In times of affliction we, like Jesus, can entrust ourselves to God's purpose confident "that in everything God works for good with those who love him, who are called according to his purpose." (Romans 8:28) As we partake of Holy Communion, we seek to become strengthened in our awareness of God's loving purpose for us.

Recently the criticism of some people hurt me deeply. I could feel my spirit sliding into the rut of self-pity and ineffectiveness. About mid-morning a young woman named Betty sought my counsel. Her best friend had spread false rumors about Betty among the people with whom Betty associated professionally and socially. Betty let this hurt defeat her. Then quite abruptly I said, "You're beautiful, you're strong, you're gifted, you're sure of success!"

Startled, she asked, "Do you really think so?"

"I am sure it is true because God has placed his image and his plan within you!" I answered.

In time she exclaimed, "God is great! With his help I do have dreams I can accomplish. I am grateful for what God can do through the heartache I face. The love of Christ will enable me to be honest with my friend who has hurt me. I'll never give up to despair!" In those moments I found God sustaining my spirit. Betty and I could rejoice in our sufferings.

Romans 5:7 can be translated, "For because of our faith in Christ he has brought us into this place of highest privilege where we now stand, and we confidently and joyfully look forward actually to become all that God has had in mind for us to be." We are as strong as the purposes we serve. Though we face adversity, we find confident joy when we know we seek by faith to serve God's highest intent for us.

2. *Become steadfast in perspective.* As we persevere in realizing God's purpose, we gain perspective on ourselves and our problems. "We rejoice in our sufferings, knowing that suffering produces endurance . . ." (Romans 5:3) The word endurance means steadfastness or perseverance. As Paul persevered through beatings, imprisonments, and sickness he gained perspective on these afflictions. He could see God working through these hardships to accomplish the divine will. A person who senses what God is doing and remains steadfast in God's purpose is able to keep all of life's events in perspective.

Abraham Lincoln's strength arose from his conviction about the just and benevolent purposes of God. Lincoln trusted God to work through times of suffering to accomplish his sovereign will. With this faith Lincoln had the steadfast perspective to endure tragedy in his family and in his nation.

Lincoln said, "I know there is a God, and that he hates injustice and slavery. I see the storm coming, and I know that his hand is in it. If he has a place and work for me — and I think he has — I believe I am ready. I am nothing, but truth is everything. I know I am right because I know that liberty is right, for Christ teaches it and Christ is God." Lincoln found the perseverance to trust God in times of affliction. Lincoln could see the tumult of his day in the light of God's purposes.

3. *Become stable in personality.* "Endurance produces character, and character produces hope, and hope does not disappoint us, because God's love has been poured into our hearts through the Holy Spirit which has been given to us." (Romans 5:4, 5) God can work through times of suffering to produce stable character. In the New Testament the words trial *(peirasmos)* and tribulation *(thilipsis)* describe the sufferings we face. Jesus spoke to his disciples saying, "You are those who have continued with me in my trials." (Luke 22:28) James said, "Count it all joy, my brethren, when you meet various trials, for . . . the testing of your faith produces steadfastness." (James 1:2, 3)

Besides trials, the New Testament says we must face tribulations. Tribulation refers to the most severe form of suffering. In Romans 5:3 this is the word translated "sufferings." "We rejoice in our sufferings" means we rejoice in our most severe afflictions. Paul said that through Christ we can rejoice even in the most severe trial because such suffering produces endurance (steadfastness) and endurance produces character. The word Paul used for character means literally "tested character." When we let Christ sustain us through times of trial, our personalities take on the strength of his Spirit.

Trials and tribulations serve to test, complete, or perfect our personalities, giving stability. I am hesitant to say that God causes a particular trial or tribulation. We can bring adversity on ourselves or we can confront suffering as a result of living in a fallen world amid rebellious people. But God can take any of our trials and tribulations and work with them to accomplish his perfect purpose for us. This faith inspires us to rejoice in our sufferings.

There is a woman who illustrates magnificently how a person can become strengthened, steadfast, and stable through suffering. I hold the highest admiration for her and asked for permission to tell her story. She wrote me:

I rejoice if my tragedies and triumphs can possibly help someone, but I have to be honest — I was not a victim, I was an overt sinner. I had choices, and I made the wrong ones. I would like to blame others, but the responsibility is mine. When I went away to school I fell into self-degrading practices. Then when I was married there was not a stable basis for that marriage. When the divorce came I thought I had reached the bottom of the pit, only to fall much deeper.

I moved into the fast lane, looking for anything to fill my unbearable loneliness and emptiness. I went so low I couldn't face myself in the mirror. After three years of hell I found my way to Covenant. One Sunday morning you talked about Jesus Christ and trusting him. Christ filled the void in my life with God's love. At last I was secure; a deep joy filled my life. I had found what I was looking for. My work was fulfilling, and I became a participant in a small group. My life became orderly and serene. I rested in this peaceful environment for three years, but the Lord had a new challenge for me and would not let me become complacent.

Today this woman holds a position which can directly impact anyone in our community in a life-or-death way. Her work and the work of those whom she directs sustain the lives of countless persons each week. Here is her description of how she struggled before accepting the new position.

The job was offered to me, but I declined. I was afraid of failure. I was comfortable and did not want the old adversities which had crushed me once before. Six months later the job was offered to me again! It began to dawn upon me that this might be a further dimension of God's plan — something that only I could do. After much prayer and agonizing, arguing and rationalizing, I happened to be in church the day you preached on 2 Timothy 2:7. "For God did not give us a spirit of fear, but a spirit of power and love and a sound mind." I knew God was trying to tell me that he would give me the courage to step out, that he wouldn't give me a job that he and I together couldn't do! He would not forsake me! I accepted the job, and it has been challenging and exciting. I only pray that I don't get in the way of what the Lord wants done.

We find the strength to overcome suffering when, first, we become strengthened in purpose, second, when we become steadfast in perspective, and third, when we become stable in personality. As we partake of the sacrament of Holy Communion we rejoice in the presence of Christ who meets us, promises to forgive our sins, and gives us his strength and joy. We now receive Christ by faith as we partake of this bread and of this cup. We rejoice in the strength he gives us to meet all events. We pray that through Christ we may become an encouragement to others.

— ***James R. Tozer***

EIGHT

What Kind of Cup Do You Bring?

1 Corinthians 10:14-22

The cup of blessing which we bless, is it not a participation in the blood of Christ? (v. 16a)

The Christian faith at times expresses itself in strange ways. It talks about persons losing their life to find it. "Whoever loses his life for my sake will find it." (Matthew 16:25b) It talks about persons finding strength through acknowledging their weaknesses. "My grace is sufficient for you, for my power is made perfect in weakness." (2 Corinthians 12:9) It talks about persons finding their freedom through bondage. "Make me a captive, Lord, and then I shall be free."

Today, as we come to the Lord's table, I would like to employ similar paradoxical imagery to express an important truth of the Christian faith. I would like to etch deeply in your minds and hearts as you come each week to worship and as you come to the Lord's table this question: What kind of cup do you bring? The answer you are able to give to that question greatly determines what you will receive of God's grace as you gather for worship and the Lord's Supper.

What kind of cup do you bring? The cup I am talking about is the receptacle of your life which is able to receive the grace and gifts God desires to give you.

What kind of cup do you bring? Some people bring a full cup. Some bring a partially filled cup. And others bring an empty cup. Let us look at what this imagery means.

I. Some people bring a cup that is already filled

It does not take much imagination to see that nothing can be added to a cup that is already full. And yet many people come to the Lord's table just that way.

Some people come with cups so full of themselves that God cannot possibly pour anything more into them. If persons perceive themselves as self-sufficient, they feel they really do not need anything from the Lord. They have all they need. Their cups are already full.

And thus it is that some people come to worship and the Lord's Supper and receive nothing. Thus it is that some people leave the sanctuary disappointed that they did not "get anything out of" the worship service. They are engaged in an exercise of futility. You cannot add anything to something already full.

What kind of cup do you bring? Is it already full?

What kind of cup do you bring?

II. Some people bring a partially filled cup

The imagery of the partially filled cup is a bit more subtle. Let me illustrate it this way. If you come to my home for a drink of iced tea and you bring your own cup already filled with a mixture of salt and alum dissolved in water, what will be the result? The iced tea will be contaminated by what is already in your cup and will not quench our thirst. Indeed the resulting mixture will bear little resemblance to the iced tea I offered you in the first place. Now this is a patently homely and ridiculous illustration; none of us would intentionally do such a thing.

And yet many of us come to worship in this way. We come with our resentments, our animosities, our bitterness, our unforgiving spirits. And we are content to let these concoctions of our spirits contaminate the gifts God pours in our cup. This is what Jesus was getting at when he advised his disciples: "If you are offering your gift at the altar, and there remember that your brother has something against you, leave your gift there before the altar and go; first be reconciled to your brother, and then come and offer your gift.'' (Matthew 5:23-24) Jesus knew that our acts of worship were useless if we allow our partially filled cups to contaminate God's gifts.

Notice that I have changed from talking about ''some people'' to talking about *us*. I belive that many more of us are guilty of coming to worship and the Lord's table with cups partially filled. It is a blind spot of people to consider themselves religious. Many things in our cups can contaminate the gifts God desires to give us — pretense, spiritual pride, self-righteousness.

What kind of cup do you bring? Is your cup partially filled? What kind of cup do you bring?

III. **Some people come with empty cups**

These persons realize their radical need for God's grace. They realize you cannot stockpile or store up God's grace. They realize that their sufficiency rests in God, not in themselves. They realize how many things in their lives contaminate the grace and gifts God desires to give to them. They realize that in order to live, and love, and serve as God intends them to do, their cups need to be constantly refilled by a never depleted source.

And so they come — we come — bringing, expecting, desperately needing our cups to be filled. And we will not be disappointed. ''Blessed are those who hunger and thirst for God and his way of life, for they shall be satisfied.'' (Matthew 5:6) Those who know themselves to be empty will be filled.

What kind of cup do you bring? Is your cup empty, waiting to be filled to overflowing?

— Carl B. Rife

NINE

Managing Our Memories

1 Corinthians 11:24-25

[Paul reports, concerning Jesus] When he had given thanks, he broke [the bread] and said, "This is my body which is for you. Do this in remembrance of me." In the same way also the cup, after supper, saying, "This cup is the new covenant in my blood. Do this, as often as you drink it, in remembrance of me."

Once again we approach the Sacrament of Holy Communion. Once again we hear Jesus say, "Do this in remembrance of me." Join me now, if you will, for a few moments as we think together about an aspect of our human life which has a very special meaning for what we are doing here today.

I speak with you about managing our memories. If I were speaking about managing a million dollars, this would not apply to everybody, because not everyone has that much money. But all of us *do* have memories; each of us, from experience and knowledge, has something to remember.

Memory is one of life's most priceless possessions. The power to remember is the golden clasp which binds together the volume of life. It is this which ties the years together and makes of them one continuous whole. It is this which makes today the total of all our yesterdays. And, of course, it is the power to remember which makes possible all learning and all personal growth.

Well, when we are remembering, what is it we are doing, actually? For one thing, we are recalling. In conversations among friends the question is often heard: "Do you recall . . .?" Do you recall this or that which happened sometime back? Do you recall this person or that whom we knew sometime ago? *Re*-call. What is it to re-call? It is to bring up from the past what is gone. It is to bring to life again in the mind something experienced or known at some previous time. And this is a priceless and precious power that we have.

Or, someone may say, "Do you recollect . . .?" Do you recollect this event or that from months or years ago? What is it to *re*-collect? It is to "collect again"; it is to bring together; it is to assemble in present mind a structure made of materials accumulated in the past — part by part, piece by piece; it is to select among these and from them construct a present. The power to recollect is a power to be treasured and cherished in every way. It is indeed a pathetic sickness when all powers of memory are gone, for instance in old age when sometimes there is no longer an ability to recall the past or recollect what has gone before.

"Remember." It is a great word. In construction work, we speak of the "frame members" of a building — joists, sills, rafters. These various members are put together to make the final structure; this is the "membering" process. To *re*-member is to member again, to put together again. In our human life the power to re-member is the ability to take the materials of the past and reassemble them in our present mind. When we are remembering, this is what we are doing. You see, memory is to have all of yesterday's materials, or many of them, in storehouse of supply ready to be called forth and become part of any day's living.

If memory is to serve us well, it serves not as a vehicle to carry us back to what was, but to bring what was forward that it may be an element, a factor, in the living present.

All of us who have lived very long have some good memories and some which are not so good. Some may be even unpleasant or bitter; and if our life is to be blessed and beautiful, it is important how we manage our memories. If we are to manage them well, we need to try to do three things.

1. The first is to practice *remembering the right things*. The Apostle Paul gives us a valuable clue to the management of our memories in Philippians 4:8: "Whatever is true, whatever is honorable, just, pure, lovely, gracious, whatever is excellent, worthy of praise, think about these things." Let your mind dwell on them, keep them up front in your thought, make them a part of your growing, ongoing self. Be selective in the thoughts to which you allocate space in your mind. Savor and cherish what is a benediction to you. Give large mind-space to what adds to the quality of your life, to what lifts you and boosts you along. In other words, arrange your memories in the order of their usefulness in achieving the higher aspirations and deeper yearnings of spirit and mind.

Bury deep the recollections of all injuries, insults, and cruelties. As your parade of memories goes by, look lovingly and longingly at the beautiful ones, but avert your gaze and let the others pass. And to the extent you can organize your own memory parade, always put the good ones up front and dress them well.

The Apostle Paul had been among the Christian folk at Philippi, and afterwards he wrote to them (1:3): "I thank my God upon every remembrance of you." It had been good to be with those people. Paul took that goodness with him, and he would never let it go.

British poet Leigh Hunt has these delightful lines:

Jenny kissed me when we met,
Leaping up from the chair she sat in.
Time, you thief, who like to get
Sweets into your list, put that in:
Say fame and fortune missed me;
But put it down that Jenny kissed me!

Don't you just love that?

We cannot always turn our memories on and off at will

like water at the kitchen sink. But we *can* practice remembering the right things; we *can* cultivate a memory for what blesses us and helps us along.

2. In the second place, it is important in the management of our memories that we practice *forgetting the things that ought to be forgotten* — those petty hurts, those misunderstandings between us and other people, those bruises and abrasions that tend to fasten themselves like parasites upon us and suck our very life away.

How sad when so much mind-space is taken up by seething cauldrons of resentment. What a tragic waste when so much life-energy is drained off by our hanging onto what should be turned loose. There is a good word for us in Job 11:6: "Forget the misery and remember it as waters that pass away." Clara Barton was once reminded of an injury cruelly inflicted upon her by someone long before. She answered, "I distinctly remember forgetting that!" I just love the spirit of that, don't you?

3. In the third place, it is important in the management of our memories that we practice *remembering the right things at the right times*. It is a mark of personal discipline to be able to call up from the past that which will be most helpful in the present moment. When we confront decisions, when we encounter temptations, when we must choose which way we will go — it is important what we remember then.

Do you recall Washington Irving's story of Rip Van Winkle? Rip has the jug of whiskey in his hand: will he drink it? If he remembers the rosy glow that followed his last drink, he probably will. But if he remembers his mother's prayers and the misery of his last hangover, he probably won't.

Driving along the public road, we are likely to be more cautious if we can remember the last grisly auto accident we saw. Simon Peter, warming himself by the fire, vehemently denied his Lord. Then, says the Scripture, he "remembered the word of Jesus and he wept." He could have spared himself a lot of agony if he had remembered sooner.

In the old days of the American camp meeting, a man knelt on the ground at the "mourner's bench" and gave his life to the Lord Christ. Later that day he drove a large wooden stake into the ground at the very spot where he had knelt, saying, "If the devil tries to tell me this isn't real, I'll bring him here, point to that stake and say, 'I know it's real; right there is where it happened!' "

Well, in the ongoing process of our living, we need to drive down some stakes, and we need to remember where they are. Always we should make the high moments as unforgettable as possible. The noble, the good, the beautiful, should be entered on memory's roster with an indelible ink that neither circumstance nor time can ever wash away.

The power to remember is one of the most significant powers we have. And great is the importance of what we remember, and when.

Now, with this understanding of memory's high role in our life's ongoing drama, may our powers of hearing be fine-tuned to listen as Jesus speaks: "Take this bread . . . Take this cup . . ." Why? He tells us: "Do this *in remembrance of me.*"

These words were spoken first by Jesus to his inner circle of disciples in that upper room in Jerusalem on the Thursday evening of his final earthly week. The next day he would die on a cross. He would be leaving them as his witnesses in the world. For them, there would be trial and danger and suffering. So he was saying to them: Wherever you go out there, whatever you do, whatever happens, I want you to remember me.

It is natural, I suppose, as one approaches death, to have a sentimental wish not to be forgotten. And one may say, "Please do not forget me when I am gone." Most of us feel a need to be remembered.

In the upper room that evening, however, it was *not* because of *his own need* to be remembered that Jesus did what he did and said what he said to those disciples. It was, rather, because of *their* need, their need to remember him. They were going to walk some difficult roads, they would face some trying times. All but one of them, apparently, would eventually be killed because of their relationship with the Lord Christ. It would not be easy to be his witnesses out there in the world; they would need every resource of guidance and strength that could possibly be theirs.

And in our world, so do we. And Jesus is saying the same thing to us that he was saying to those other disciples long ago: I want you to remember me. When you are struggling with temptation, he is saying, I want you to remember me, how I was "tempted at all points as you are, yet without sin." When the road ahead is dark, he is saying, when the path to take is unclear and the footing is unsure, I want you to remember me — and never to forget that "I am the way, and the truth, and the life." When the weight of your sin settles upon you as a burden too heavy to bear, he is saying, I want you to remember me and the cross on which I have borne your sins and the sins of the whole world.

Jesus is saying: Before you decide to profane that precious life of yours, remember me, and understand how I have valued you. Before you consent to the power of evil *around* you, remember me and the power I give *within* you, remember me and the forgiveness of sin which I am forever offering to you. And lest at last you should stand in weakness trembling at the intimidating prospect of death, remember me and know that "I am the resurrection and the life" and that they who "live and believe in me shall never die," not really.

If you and I who know the Christ can remember him at all times, in all circumstances, under all conditions, then these lives of ours will never, never, go very far wrong. Of all the memories which play across the stage of today's living, let us be sure that the remembrance of our Lord Christ is up front and center. Among the many "right things" for which we should cultivate a memory, nothing can ever be more ''right'' than the remembrance of him who is our Savior. There will never be a time or circumstance in which you or I will not be helped by remembering him.

And so, knowing of *our great need* of remembering him, Jesus gives to us these symbols of his broken body and shed blood, saying, ''Do this'' as a perpetual reminder of me. To his disciples in that upper room, Jesus said, ''Do this,'' and when you see me die on a cross tomorrow, remember. ''Do this,'' and when in the after-years you are put to suffering for your faith, then remember.

To *us*, to you and me here today, to his disciples of this present place and time, he says, ''Do this,'' and when you go out into the living of your tomorrows, whatever they bring, whatever happens, whatever comes, then remember me. In the complicated maze of possible roads you may take, remembering, make choice of what is right. In the fierce struggles with trouble and pain, remembering, be strong. And, he is saying, I am the Christ triumphant, and you are mine; remember the victories I promise you; rejoice and be glad.

In the Sacrament of Holy Communion, you understand, Christ is asking us to use one of our finest powers as a safeguard of life's highest and best and as a guide to life's noblest goals. He is asking us to marshall the full powers of memory and employ them as a resource of guidance and strength. He is appealing to us, as we arrange our memory banks, to give a large place to the remembrance of him — today and every day, here and everywhere.

— Leonard W. Mann

TEN

The Sermon in the Supper

1 Corinthians 11:26

For as often as you eat this bread and drink the cup, you proclaim the Lord's death until he comes.

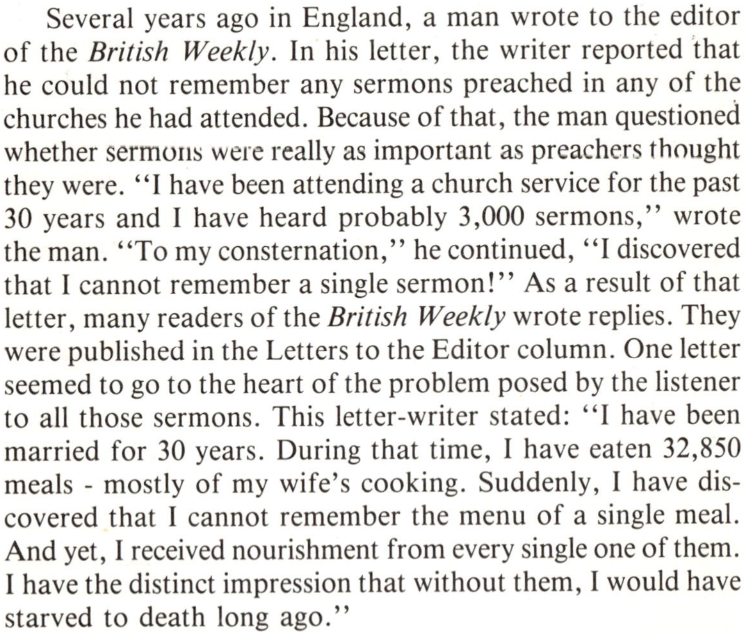

Several years ago in England, a man wrote to the editor of the *British Weekly*. In his letter, the writer reported that he could not remember any sermons preached in any of the churches he had attended. Because of that, the man questioned whether sermons were really as important as preachers thought they were. "I have been attending a church service for the past 30 years and I have heard probably 3,000 sermons," wrote the man. "To my consternation," he continued, "I discovered that I cannot remember a single sermon!" As a result of that letter, many readers of the *British Weekly* wrote replies. They were published in the Letters to the Editor column. One letter seemed to go to the heart of the problem posed by the listener to all those sermons. This letter-writer stated: "I have been married for 30 years. During that time, I have eaten 32,850 meals - mostly of my wife's cooking. Suddenly, I have discovered that I cannot remember the menu of a single meal. And yet, I received nourishment from every single one of them. I have the distinct impression that without them, I would have starved to death long ago."

Week after week, sermons are preached in churches around the Christian world. While most of those who mount the pulpit pray for divine inspiration, the sermons they preach may be gripping or boring, depending on the ingenuity, resourcefulness, and talents of the preacher. God would certainly not leave the message of the Gospel to the frailties of human preachers alone. And we have in recent times seen how frail those human preachers can be! God made sure that despite human inadequacies, his message would not be lost. On the night before his death, Jesus Christ gave us the Sacrament of the Lord's Supper. It is known by other names, too: the Holy Communion; the Eucharist; the Mass; the Divine Liturgy. Writing about this holy Sacrament, Saint Paul said: "For every time you eat this bread and drink this cup you are retelling the message of the Lord's death, that he died for you. Do this until he comes again." (1 Corinthians 11:26, The Living Bible) Above and beyond the sermons in our pulpits, there is a Sermon in the Supper!

I

The Sermon in the Supper is a message about a Person. Edward Bok was an American journalist who became editor of *Ladies' Home Journal* in 1889. In 1891, he was elected vice-president of the Curtis Publishing Company, which published the magazine. For 30 years, Edward Bok and the *Journal* worked for such causes as the better-babies movement, teaching social hygiene to children, beautifying American cities, and improving home architecture. Bok recounted that he always kept the memory of the death of his mother sacred. April 30 was the anniversary of her death. Each year on that date, at 3:20 p.m. in the afternoon, Bok always took out his watch and thought of her, regardless of what he was then doing or where he was at the time. On one of the anniversaries of her death, Bok was with some of his friends. He saw that the time of his mother's death was drawing near. He became quiet, thoughtful, and finally withdrew to one side of the room. Lost in his thoughts, he lived over again some of the experiences he had enjoyed with his mother. When he returned to the table where his friends were sitting, one of them said, "Do you know, you looked exactly like your mother just now when you were standing over there by the wall." Bok replied, "Yes, I was thinking about her."

The Sacrament of the Holy Communion tells us about the Person who is at the center of our Faith. That Person is Jesus Christ. As we live in holy communion with the Person of Christ, we tend to grow into his likeness. Think of some home you know where a husband and wife have loved one another and lived together for many years. Sharing ideas, developing common tastes, experiencing common feelings, they have come to resemble one another. This is the fact to which Saint Paul pointed in the third chapter of his second letter to the Corinthians: "We all reflect as in a mirror the splendour of the Lord; thus we are transfigured into his likeness, from splendour to splendour." (2 Corinthians 3:18, New English Bible) Henry Drummond paraphrased Paul's words in this way: "We all reflecting as a mirror the character of Christ are transformed into the same Image from character to character." Every time you come to church and receive the bread and wine, you are proclaiming the death of that Person in whose likeness we are to be shaped. "For from the very beginning God decided that those who came to him . . . should become like his Son, so that his Son would be the First, with many brothers." (Romans 8:29, The Living Bible)

II

The Sermon in the Supper is a message about a Passion. The word "passion" means a very strong feeling. When the word "passion" is used about Jesus Christ, it refers to his sufferings in the Garden of Gethsemane and on the cross of Golgotha. The bread and wine of the Sacrament tell us again and again about the passionate love of Jesus Christ for us. Think about the piece of bread that is placed in your hands when you come to church to receive this holy Sacrament. Bread is made from many grains of wheat. This wheat had to pass through the adversities of winter. It had to be put under pressure and ground beneath a millstone. It had to go through fire before it became bread. Think about the wine you sip when you come to church to receive the Lord's Supper. This wine was made from many grapes. To become wine, those grapes, too, suffered, as it were, by having their life crushed from them. It is because the elements of bread and wine endure such rigors that they symbolize for us the Passion and sufferings of Christ.

William Temple was a priest of the Church of England who became Archbishop of Canterbury in April, 1942 and served until October, 1944. In one of his books, Archbishop Temple wrote: "Men say, 'There cannot be a God of love, because if there were, and he looked upon this world, his heart would break.' The Church," replied Temple, "points to the cross and says: 'His heart *does* break.' Men say, 'It is God who has made the world. It is He who is responsible, and it is He who should bear the load.' The church points to the cross, and says, 'He *does* bear it.' "

In one of his books, Dr. Leslie Weatherhead recalled a night when his ship sailed past the island of Stromboli, off the coast of Sicily. He saw the bright fires of the Strombolian volcano light up the black sky. "Just as the flash of the volcano reveals the fires forever burning in the mountain's heart," wrote Dr. Weatherhead, "so the incident [on the cross of Christ] on Calvary two thousand years ago shows the nature of the eternal God."

I sometimes think about the Cross,
And shut my eyes and try to see
The cruel nails and crown of thorns,
And Jesus crucified for me.

But even could I see Him die,
I could but see a little part
Of that great love which like a fire
Is always burning in His heart.

Every time you come to church and receive the bread and wine, you are proclaiming the Passion of that Person in whom we see the human face of God. The Sacrament announces the message of the Cross, telling us, in Leslie Brandt's inspired phrase, "the high cost of loving!"

III

The Sermon in the Supper is a message about a Promise. After telling his Corinthian friends that by the actions of eating and drinking, they were retelling the message of Christ's death, Paul wrote, "Do this until he comes again." (1 Corinthians 11:26, The Living Bible) Those first Christians lived under the spell of Christ's promise to come again. In his book *The Theology of Jewish Christianity*, Jean Danielou, a Roman Catholic scholar, argues that the symbolism of the star in the Book of Numbers ("A star shall come forth out of Jacob," Numbers 24:17, NEB) was transformed into a Cross of Light. Danielou is referring to "the Cross of Light" mentioned in the apocryphal Gospel of Peter. In this book, the Cross of Light was said to have accompanied Christ in his ascent into heaven. It was expected to precede him at his coming again. For that reason, it became the custom in the early days of the church for Christians to paint a cross on the eastern wall of their homes and their meeting places. This cross was not simply put on the wall to remind them of the sufferings of Christ which had happened in the past. On the contrary, the sign of the cross was placed on that particular wall to mark the East from which Christ was expected to come again in power and great glory. Christians in later times would forget the original reason why the cross was placed on the east wall. They did not know that it was an emblem of the future from which "the bright Star of Dawn" (Revelation 22:16, NEB) would appear. Because they had lost this sense of the forward look, they made the cross exclusively a memorial of Christ's death in the past.

The Sacrament of the Holy Communion tells us about the Promise of Christ to return. Though men may forget that the Cross has this future aspect, God made sure that this element of Faith would not be forever forgotten. The Sacrament of the Lord's Supper tells us the message: "I shall come again and receive you to myself, so that where I am you may be also." (John 14:3, NEB)

The Lord's Supper is an acted sermon in which the message of Christ's death is retold as it is commemorated. As we receive the bread and drink from the cup, we are announcing our love for the Person of Christ, our remembrance of the Passion of Christ, and our anticipation of the Promise of Christ.

— *Edward Chinn*

The Lord's Supper is a Sermon
we act out — In it the Message
of X's death is remembered & retold.
As each of us receive the Bread & ~~the~~
drink from the Cup, we are stating our
love for the the Person of X
Proclaiming Our remembrance of
the passion of X.
And Our anticipation of the
promised return of X.

ELEVEN

Come, Learn Your Worth

2 Corinthians 5:15-21

Therefore, if any [are] in Christ, [they are] new creation[s]; the old has passed away, behold, the new has come. (v. 17)

John Bishop tells of a London slum child whose major refuge was his Roman Catholic day school. In the course of things, his school was visited by a physician who did medical examinations for the students. As the skinny little fellow left the doctor's room, one of the nuns asked, "Well, Jimmy, what did the doctor say to you?"

Jimmy answered, "He took one look at me and said, 'What a miserable specimen you are!' " Now the boy paused for a moment and his face brightened. "But he didn't know that I'd had my first Communion, did he, Sister?"

Perhaps that story will strike you as little more than a quaint bit of sentiment. I report it, however, as a profound declaration of hope for us human creatures. We need to know what we're worth. And sometimes, Lord help us, we need simply to know that we're worth *something*!

We live in a world where, as you know, it's difficult to realize our worth. Daily headlines tell us that life is cheap. If thousands die through violence and millions through neglect and malnutrition, life must indeed put a cheap price on us. And it's such a big world; how can we seem to have any worth when we are one in four billion? If one of us stops breathing, how much difference does it make in the totality of things? Then, too, there's the distortion in our human values: if scoundrels grow rich peddling dope while nurses are paid modestly for saving lives, then what is the value of a human being?

Mind you, we are often told some measures of our worth, but too often those measures have a way of leaving us diminished. Someone, in the common language of measurement, says of a person, "He must be worth at least a million." But if the person described is astute, he has to think to himself, "Is that all I'm worth? Suppose I lose that million, in a change in the fortunes of the market: then I'm not worth a thing."

So often it seems that people estimate our worth on the basis of things which can change; and because others measure us that way, we're inclined to make the same kind of measure. Some have the impression (and society encourages it) that it is their youthfulness which makes them desirable. So what happens, then, when youth is replaced by lines in the face and sags in the body? If our worth lies in being young, where is our worth when youth goes?

Or suppose our worth seems to rest in some skill or achievement, even a very worthy one. A concert pianist or violinist may enjoy the feeling of artistic achievement, and with it, public acclaim. But if one day arthritis diminishes the dexterity of the performer's fingers, is her worth gone, too? So often society (and we, in turn) judges our worth by measures which time can change.

No wonder, then, that fear and bitterness sometimes intrude upon us in this question of worth. A young wife loves to hear her husband extol her beauty; but forgive her if she sometimes wonders if he will still find her so desirable when her figure has less winsome lines. An athlete exults in the thunders of applause when he catches the game-winning pass. But next week he drops the ball and the game is lost, and those who cheered so recently seem now to have been replaced in the stadium by a new crowd who fiercely call for him to be benched. A politician wins big and everyone adores him; then a faux pas or two, and he is rejected by an even greater margin than in his former victory. It's no wonder that old-timers in sports, politics and entertainment say cynically, "They love you when you're up, but brother, they don't even know you when you're down."

Nor is it too surprising, then, that sometimes people who seem to have a great deal going for them are unsure of their worth. Often, as a pastoral counselor, I have talked with some young man or woman who is healthy, bright, attractive — and with it all, self-despising. I've reasoned with them: "How can you look at your grade point and think anything but good of yourself? Or how can you look in the mirror without saying, 'Wow, I'm terrific!'?" But all that surface worth is undercut by a feeling that the person down below the looks, personality and grades is not really loved or appreciated. Strip me, they think, of these things, and would anybody care much about what's left? What am I worth, below the surface which people see?

No wonder, then, that we sometimes do perverse and stupid things to seek affirmation of our worth. The child that throws a tantrum, the teenager in rebellion, the husband who barks and grumbles all day Saturday, the hypochondriac who never tires of reciting her imagined ills: these may only be trying to get someone to pay more attention to them, to assure them that they have value.

So I stand today at this table of holy communion and extend an invitation: *Come to this table, and learn your worth.*

Almost immediately I think I hear someone saying, "But in a communion service, we are told that we are sinners. You know — it says something like, 'Ye that do truly and earnestly repent of your sins.' And there's even a special place for confessing our sins. How can it help us feel our worth when it makes so much of our sins?"

I'm glad you've asked that question, because that's really my first point. You can't know your worth unless someone takes you seriously. I think of a little child bringing a crayon drawing to an adult who looks just long enough to say, "Oh, that's beautiful, honey, just beautiful." It's not a compliment, because the adult isn't taking the child seriously. Which is too say that thoughtless praise isn't praise at all. Rather, it's the ultimate insult, because it says that the person doesn't really matter. I think of a seminary professor who wrote no comments on term papers and offered no grade; he simply put a check mark in the corner to indicate he had seen the paper. I dreaded writing for him because I didn't feel he took me seriously. By contrast I remember a professor in graduate school who often wrote scathing comments about grammar, logic and scholarship, in half-a-dozen different colors. He called it "rainbow treatment." While I smarted under the vigor of his criticism, I cherished that professor. I knew he cared enough about me to demand my best.

The communion service reminds me that God cares about me. My sins trouble him. He doesn't wink at them, nor does he pat me patronizingly and say, "They don't really matter." Nothing so much diminishes a person — child, spouse or friend — as to be told, "I don't care what you do." I learn something of my worth at the communion table because it calls me to repentance. This service reminds me that God is in earnest about me.

That is, I am complimented by the very fact that I am capable of sin. When the communion ritual asks me to repent, it reminds me that I have the capacity for decision. I am no puppet, acting from pulled strings; I am no animal, responding helplessly to instincts; I am a human being, able to choose between right and wrong. If I were incapable of wrong, my stature would be next to nothing. But the communion ritual pays me the honor of declaring that I am capable of doing wrong, and it insists that I am able also to do right, and that I ought therefore to be sorry for any wrong I do. And above all else, it tells me that God thinks so highly of me that he is upset by my wrongdoing.

But the communion service says a still greater thing: that

Jesus Christ died for our sins. As Saint Paul put it, "For our sake God made him to be sin who knew no sin, so that in him we might become the righteousness of God."[1] Here is the most dramatic evidence of our worth: Christ died for us. The Ultimate One made the ultimate sacrifice. In our common world our worth is often measured on the basis of who will stand up for us, or speak in our behalf. In juvenile court, for instance, a youngster is sometimes spared if a responsible citizen will vouch for him. Then hear this: the Christian Gospel declares that Jesus Christ has not only spoken for us, he has *acted* for us, and has acted decisively.

Some of you may remember the name of Muretus. He was a poor, wandering scholar in the Middle Ages. He became ill while in an Italian town, and was taken to a hospital for strays and helpless creatures. The doctors discussed his case in Latin — a mark of learned men in those times — never thinking that this nondescript begger would understand. One of them suggested that since he was only a worthless wanderer, they might well use him for medical experiments. Muretus looked up and answered in their own learned Latin: "Call no man worthless for whom Christ died."

Here, indeed, is the measure of our worth. However much of a failure we may have been, God — who knows us best — thinks us worth the death of his Son. Could there be better evidence of our worth? Sometimes life lays us low and like Muretus we hear the analysts of the world muttering their mumbo-jumbo over us. "An average I.Q.," one voice says. "A bit psychotic," another answers. "Given to delusions of grandeur." "A failed marriage." "Captive to his glands and instincts." And to all of this heaven answers, "She is of such worth that my Son became sin for her and died on her behalf."

The communion table affirms our worth; indeed, shouts it. In a world of four billion people, this table says that you are singular; there is no one else like you. In a culture that can easily cast you aside when you are too old, too slow, or too ordinary, this table says that your age, your speed of mind or body, and your appearance does not matter. God loves you

[1] 2 Corinthians 5:21 (RSV)

for what you *are*, for the intrinsic, ineffaceable worth of you. Sometimes, in the press of living, we get so we don't even like ourselves. We grow tired of our own failings and even of our own best strivings. We need no one else to depreciate us because we have already downgraded ourselves. And just then this table declares, "You are one for whom Christ died. How dare you think badly of yourself when God thinks so ultimately well of you? How is your opinion of yourself to be compared with his opinion of you?"

The Apostle Paul makes a grand insistence. "From now on," he writes, "we regard no one from a human point of view . . . if any one is in Christ, he is a new creation . . ."[2] I must look at each person, including myself, as one whom God loves and for whom Christ died. I must know that every person is capable of becoming a new creation. A person's worth is very great if he is able, through Christ, to become a new creature.

Those of Scottish heritage may know a familiar tale which is said to have begun with the MacDonald clan. Donald Gorm was in London and was asked to the Lord Mayor's Banquet. But they set him rather near the wrong side of the salt, as if he were nothing more than a country squire. Midway through the banquet, someone told the host that Gorm was actually a great prince in his own country, and that at that very moment he was negotiating a treaty with King Henry VIII.

The Lord Mayor quickly sent a messenger to invite Donald Gorm to sit at his right hand. Gorm's reply is legendary. "Tell the Lord Mayor not to be fashing himself. Wherever MacDonald is sitting, that is the head of the table."

Such is our mood this morning as we kneel at the table of the Lord. Whether you or the world about you sees you or me as success or failure, whether we feel pretty or ordinary, whether we are solvent or destitute, hear this: Where Jesus Christ sits, is the head of the table; and he has chosen that you and I sit next to him.

Come to this Table, my friend, and learn your worth.

— *J. Ellsworth Kalas*

[2] 2 Corinthians 5:16a, 17a (RSV)

TWELVE

The Ministry of Refreshing

2 Timothy 1:16-19

> *May the Lord grant mercy to the household of Onesiphorus, for he often refreshed me; he was not ashamed of my chains . . . (v. 16)*

Meet Onesiphorus.

Onesiphorus was a friend of Saint Paul's. We ought to think about him. We ought to imitate him.

Saint Paul writes about Onesiphorus in his second letter to Timothy. Paul's letters make up about a third of the entire New Testament. They are theological treasuries. For sublime thought, for spiritual energy, for powerful theology, they are probably without equal in Christian literature.

But they are letters, and as with all letters, in some ways the most interesting parts are the personal touches. Often Paul had to write with disappointment of the many fair-weather friends who deserted him in time of trouble. Often Paul had to warn against enemies who were out to burn him and other Christians. But other times Paul could write of those persons who did him great kindnesses. One of these is Onesiphorus.

This is what Paul, in chains in a Roman prison, writes to Timothy about Onesiphorus:

> *You are aware that all who are in Asia turned away from me, and among them Phygelus and Herogenes. May the Lord grant mercy to the household of Onesiphorus, for* he often refreshed me; *he was not ashamed of my chains, but when he arrived in Rome he searched for me eagerly and found*

me — may the Lord grant him to find mercy from the Lord on that Day — and you well know all the service he rendered at Ephesus.

Timothy may have known, but we don't know what service Onesiphorus rendered at Ephesus. We *do* know, however, that he "often refreshed" Paul in Rome.

Paul is one of the great men of history. Yet the less known man could and did minister to the greater man, refreshed him, helped restore his soul, gave him renewed strength for the struggle.

What sort of person was Onesiphorus? He had a record for service. His friendship wasn't put off by the socially embarrassing, or perhaps even personally dangerous fact that Paul was in prison. Instead, he went out of his way eagerly to find his friend. What they talked about there in Paul's cell, what word Onesiphorus had to say, we can only guess. But as a result of Onesiphorus' visits, Paul felt brightened, cheered, rekindled: "He often refreshed me."

I think we can understand that. We all know activities, situations, and persons that drain off our energy. There are people whom to be with is an utterly exhausting experience. They exude a miasma that makes you wilt.

But if we are fortunate to have a friend like Onesiphorus, we also know people who build us up, who recharge our batteries. Then we may find ourselves saying, "The other day I was heavy-hearted," or, "I was low in spirit," or "I was weary," or any equivalent of confessing that we were in a spiritual prison, "and you, my friend, — perhaps not by any particular thing you said or did, but just by your Christian attitude of love and understanding, by your eagerly going out of your way to find me — you were the instrument by whom God restored my soul. You refreshed me. You helped me to make it through." And perhaps our friend will even say, "When did I help you? Our friend may not remember, but we do, with great gratitude. We thank God for sending us ministers of refreshment.

These are people like Onesiphorus. These are the spiritual Gunga Dins.

From Rudyard Kipling's poem or from a movie, everyone remembers Gunga Din. Gunga Din was a water carrier attached to the British army in India. Gunga Din and his brothers were important parts of the fighting forces. In the heat of battle in that dry land, it was their job to carry the water around to thirsty men. Some of them displayed great courage as they performed their dangerous errands of mercy. A little imagination paints the scene: blazing sun, burning sand, gunsmoke, shells, bullets, wounded and dying men, and the water carriers. No wonder they were immortalized in poetry and song.

Spiritually, it's not far from that scene to the scene Saint Mark describes at Golgotha, where Jesus on the cross was dying a lingering death by exposure to the sun's blast and self-suffocation — I was about to say "an excruciating death," but we get that word *excruciating* from the word for cross; that's exactly what it means. And Jesus cries out, "I thirst! I thirst!" And Saint Mark reports, "And one ran" — *ran* — to get something moist to hold to the parched lips of Jesus.

There ran the spiritual ancestor of Gunga Din and Onesiphorus and all the other ministers of refreshing. Of all that crowd who stood around the cross with vengeful, hate-filled hearts, or with uncaring curiosity, beholding Christ's agony, here was one person who ran to do some little thing to relieve his thirst. If ever one small, anonymous act of kindness made someone blessed of God, surely that was it. "I was thirsty and you gave me drink." I love the person who that day ran and did that for my dying Lord.

The Bible reminds us constantly that God has all along been using spiritual water carriers in the ministry of refreshment, from the rock which gave the Hebrew children water on their toilsome way through the wilderness, to the seer's vision of the river of life flowing from a sea like crystal surrounding the throne of God.

Who can forget the story of King David, parched from the

heat of battle. Two soldiers crawled through no-man's land to bring their beloved leader water. Humbled and lifted by the love of friends who would risk their lives to refresh him — and recognizing that such love had transformed that cup into an outward and visible sign of an inward and spiritual grace — David knew that he could never drink it for his own need. That water had become so pure that he could offer it only as a sacrifice to God. Was he still thirsty? His tongue and throat, yes, but that love had refreshed his spirit, restored his soul.

James Russell Lowell knew that it was the personal touch which transformed a cup of water into the Holy Grail — "The gift without the giver is bare." Onesiphorus went out of his way eagerly to seek Paul out. Whatever words Onesiphorus might have said, his self-giving alone would have lifted Paul's spirit.

In Berthold Brecht's play, *The Good Woman of Setzuan*, Wong, the water-seller, has a hard life. When water is scarce, he has to go a long and difficult way to fetch the water; when water is plentiful, he has no income. Shen Te, the "Good Woman," meets an aviator and falls in love. To celebrate her love, she wants to buy her flyer a cup of water, so she goes running to Wong in the rain. Wong says, bitterly, "Throw back your head and open your mouth and you'll have all the water you need."

But Shen Te says tenderly:

I want your *water, Wong*
The water that has tired you so
The water that you carried all this way
*The water that is hard to sell because it's been raining.**

So we see how the mere substance of H_2O alone is not enough, and that God has always used spiritual Gunga Dins and good persons in the personal ministry of refreshment.

It's a major reason we're in worship each Sunday. We find God to be the wellspring of living water who never fails to renew the strength of those who wait upon him.

* Berthold Brecht, *The Good Woman of Setzuan,* Grove Press, Inc., New York, 1966, pp. 60, 61.

The connection with the service of communion is clear. By the sacrifice he made of himself Jesus — our Servant Lord who taught us that whoever would be great among us should also be a servant — Jesus has transformed this cup into a sacrament of God's love. We drink this cup — not water or even mere wine, but the blood, that is to say, the very person, the life of Christ, of love itself — in remembrance that Christ gave his life for us, and we are thankful. Our souls are restored.

If we love him, we will feed his sheep. Refreshed, we will become ministers of refreshment. It is an important assignment in the army of God. It is an act in which God bestows blessing.

Soon we'll unite in this simple act. We'll sip. With scarcely enough to moisten the lips, we'll drink refreshment for our souls. It's so much more than a mere ritual act! It's a sacrament, brought to us by Christ's sacrifice for our sakes to renew life within us for his sake and for the sake of his little ones.

Let me make a prayer for all of us as we commune. It's simply this: that, as we are refreshed, God will grant us grace that we may become persons who refresh others who thirst. In our daily round of duties and activities, in our home life, may we become more sharply aware of the needs of those about us, of the painful if often hidden ways in which their souls may thirst after some word of concern, of understanding, of encouragement, of loyalty, of love. In the heat of life's battle, may we bring the refreshing of God's love.

May someone have cause to say of us, "He or she often refreshed me."

We may one day be surprised with joy to hear our Master say, "I was thirsty, and you gave me drink."

"Lord, when saw we thee thirsty and gave thee drink?"

"Inasmuch as you did it unto one of the least of these my brethren, you have done it unto me."

— ***Robert John Versteeg***

THIRTEEN

The Gathering, The Scattering

Hebrews 10:22-24

Let us draw near with a true heart in full assurance of faith, with our hearts sprinkled clean . . . (v. 22a)
. . . Stir up one another to love and good works. (v. 24b)

It's right there, in the name itself: comm*union* — that which makes for unity, oneness. But if this Christian sacrament of unity has been anything through twenty centuries, it has been a sacrament of division.

Let's move backward quickly through those centuries, taking snapshots as we go.

Frame 1. Christians visit in the parish of a sister congregation whose denominational roots are identical to their own. But they are forbidden to come to the altar because "there is doctrinal divergence between us."

Frame 2. A stormy meeting of the congregation ends by silencing members of the worship committee who hoped to offer the Sacrament of the Altar at every worship service. The argument that clinched the vote: "You make a special thing too common and before you know it nobody will come to take it any more." Members of the silenced task-force fall to wondering whether the same would be true for the eating of regular meals each day, but decide not to raise the point publicly and risk further acrimony.

Frame 3. Martin Luther and Ulrich Zwingli scowl at one another from either end of a long banquet table at Castle Coburg in Central Germany. They cannot agree about what "Hoc est . . ." really means. As Luther smashes his fist down on the table-top, making the salt shakers jump six inches, all hope dies for one great unified church of the Reformation.

Frame 4. Fearful that they may dishonor Jesus' actual blood and body, medieval Christians only come to take the sacrament when absolutely necessary. To preclude, their violating it, the priest withholds the wine and will no longer put the bread directly into each one's hands.

Frame 5. Christians gather for a love feast in a private home in Corinth. The first ones there drink all the wine and stagger, drunk, about the room before the liturgy has even started.

1. Holy Communion Gathers Us

What was Jesus really after when, that night at supper, he announced a brand new covenant in bread and wine? Clearly, the meaning is multi-dimensional. There is something of the Passover from Egypt in what happened at that table. Clearly, animal sacrifice was reinterpreted and invested with a new and hair-raising meaning. Clearly, what was next to happen on the Cross was here anticipated and in some incredible and mysterious way drawn from Friday afternoon back into Thursday night. A wonderful prolepsis — drawing the future into the present — was occurring.

But in spite of, and along with, all those meanings, one thing seems transparently clear. The meal which was that night established was intended to provide the occasion for a fellowship, a sharing, a new unity of heart and mind and spirit that the followers of Jesus had not known before.

Imagine a swimming pool. There is a high chain-link fence round about it. A gatekeeper screens swimmers. On the inside, splashing and refreshing one another in the scorching heat of summer, are a couple dozen lucky individuals. It is a private pool party. Beyond them, looking through the fence, their swimming suits on but with no invitation, the less-than-lucky stand, their fingers curled into the fence, their bodies eager for the coolness of the water.

"Come on in," somebody shouts from somewhere in the pool. "The water's great!" But others in the water grumble. "Them? They're black (or white or red or brown or yellow). We don't know them. There's not room in here. It's cozy as it is. Don't spoil it!"

Now the party host climbs up to pool-side. To the gate he goes. He whispers in the ear of the gatekeeper. In ten seconds the pool is wide open. Everybody may come in.

Among the original guests, there's confusion. Some leave in a huff. Some scowl, but stay. Some welcome strangers to their midst. Before an hour is past, a grand time is enjoyed by all.

For weary bodies, hearts and souls, the Lord Christ opens his refreshing swimming pool, his holy meal, his gracious future, to the world. He says, "Draw near . . ."

It has sometimes been said that if we cannot embrace one another, we ought not pretend to share the unity the sacramental meal holds out to us. Imagine people at a pool party, fastidiously trying not to bump into each other or to graze each other's shoulders, since they cannot really stand each other. Jesus says, "Draw near . . ." He means not only to invite us to the meal, the party, but that we also draw near to each other. What better way to prepare for this meal than to exchange a word of peace, and shake a hand — or even to embrace — as some of our church liturgies prescribe these days? In Paul's day there was something called a "holy kiss." You will not kiss someone you cannot stand.

We do not know entirely what this special meal is all about. We *do* know that it is a time for unity. "Draw near," the host invites. "Draw near to me . . . let me draw near to you (and, in the eating and the drinking, let me come *within you*) . . . and draw near to one another.

Do you realize that individual next to you here at the alter is about to lose her job? Can you embrace that person in some helpful way? Draw near . . .

That man who kneels there at your other side. He sees his marriage failing. Can you empathize? Draw near . . .

The pastor who is serving you the bread. His daughter has repudiated all her father taught her and is living with her boyfriend now. Who can embrace the pastor in his grief just now? Draw near to him . . .

2. Holy Communion Scatters Us

And when the party's over, as the sun begins to tip, we leave the pool, remove our soggy swimwear, towel our hair dry, and head out, refreshed, to opportunities and battles waiting for us. Maybe we go back to where we started with new friends because the party was expanded.

Maybe wc go out with thoughts of the next opportunity to dive into a cooling pool the next time (and, we hope, that time will not be far away). Maybe we have learned some things about the others with whom we enjoyed the party, things we never would have known in other contexts. We remember a wise maxim, posted at the door of a gymnasium: "I learn more about you if I play one hour with you than I would learn by talking with you for a month."

"Let us consider how to stir up one another to love and good works," the writer of the Book of Hebrews admonishes. What does the party, or the meal, mean to us when we've found the unity we seek, the strength, the energy, and the refreshment needed for the days which follow?

Parties, meals, and times of unity lose all their meaning if we cannot scatter once the gathering is through. And when we scatter, we take from that special time the opportunities they build into us — opportunities to share the celebration we've experienced with the ones we know and meet and touch, who could not share the party or the meal.

The Lord who loved us into coming to that meal, that party, loved us with a powerful embrace while we were there with him. He sends us with that love into the world, to spread and share the fruits of unity by loving those who could not come.

Where are they whom we scatter to embrace?

• They're people we are married to.

• They're those with whom we share our daily bread each suppertime.

• They're those who ride the bus with us, or drive the streets and freeways we must travel.

• They're where we buy our groceries, pay our rent, or pump our gas.

• They're hidden from our view until we look for them. They're children of the Heavenly Father. They are those who need a hug, a warm embrace, the nourishment that only those first strengthened at the table, or refreshed at God's pool party, can impart.

Lord, gather us. Unite us. Feed us and refresh us. Then, Lord, scatter us, to share with all whom we know and meet the wonders of your grace.

— Michael L. Sherer

Contributors

Edward Chinn is pastor of All Saints' Episcopal Church in Philadelphia, Pennsylvania.

Carl L. Jech, an ordained Lutheran pastor, teaches philosophy, religion and humanities in the San Francisco Bay Area.

J. Ellsworth Kalas has for seventeen years served The Church of the Saviour (United Methodist) in Cleveland, Ohio.

Wallace H. Kirby is District Superintendent for the United Methodist Church's Durham, North Carolina, District.

Leonard W. Mann is a United Methodist pastor living in retirement in Lancaster, Ohio.

Thomas D. Peterson is a United Methodist pastor living in retirement in Saratoga Springs, New York.

Carl B. Rife is pastor of Milford Mill United Methodist Church, Baltimore, Maryland.

Michael L. Sherer is pastor of Trinity Lutheran Church, Elida, Ohio.

James R. Tozer is pastor of Covenant Presbyterian Church, West Lafayette, Indiana.

Robert John Versteeg is pastor of Oak Hills United Methodist Church, Cincinnati, Ohio.